50 Delicious Fruit Dessert Recipes for Home

By: Kelly Johnson

Table of Contents

- Classic Apple Pie
- Peach Cobbler
- Blueberry Crisp
- Strawberry Shortcake
- Raspberry Tart
- Pineapple Upside-Down Cake
- Mango Sorbet
- Kiwi Lime Pie
- Grapefruit Bars
- Watermelon Granita
- Lemon Meringue Pie
- Blackberry Crumble
- Cherry Clafoutis
- Pear Frangipane Tart
- Plum Galette
- Banana Bread
- Coconut Macaroons with Pineapple
- Orange Almond Cake
- Fig and Honey Cheesecake
- Cranberry Orange Bread
- Mixed Berry Fool
- Apple Crisp Bars
- Grilled Peaches with Honey and Mascarpone
- Strawberry Rhubarb Crisp
- Pineapple Coconut Tiramisu
- Mango Sticky Rice
- Raspberry Lemon Bars
- Blueberry Lemon Bundt Cake
- Pear Gingerbread Cake
- Blackberry Pie Bars
- Peach Melba
- Apricot Galette
- Grapefruit Sorbet
- Lemon Poppy Seed Cake
- Cherry Chocolate Chip Cookies

- Watermelon Sorbet
- Kiwi Pavlova
- Banana Pudding
- Coconut Lime Bars
- Orange Creamsicle Pie
- Mango Coconut Rice Pudding
- Raspberry Swirl Cheesecake
- Strawberry Balsamic Ice Cream
- Pineapple Coconut Crisp
- Blackberry Lime Cupcakes
- Peach Melba Crumble
- Blueberry Lemon Scones
- Mango Raspberry Popsicles
- Raspberry Chocolate Tart
- Mixed Berry Bread Pudding

Classic Apple Pie

Ingredients:

For the Pie Crust:

- 2 1/2 cups all-purpose flour
- 1 teaspoon salt
- 1 tablespoon granulated sugar
- 1 cup unsalted butter, cold and cubed
- 6-8 tablespoons ice water

For the Apple Filling:

- 6-7 medium apples (such as Granny Smith, Honeycrisp, or Fuji), peeled, cored, and thinly sliced
- 1/2 cup granulated sugar
- 1/4 cup packed light brown sugar
- 2 tablespoons all-purpose flour
- 1 teaspoon ground cinnamon
- 1/4 teaspoon ground nutmeg
- 1 tablespoon lemon juice
- 1 tablespoon unsalted butter, cut into small pieces

For Assembly:

- 1 egg, beaten (for egg wash)
- 1 tablespoon granulated sugar (for sprinkling)

Instructions:

For the Pie Crust:

1. In a large mixing bowl, whisk together the flour, salt, and granulated sugar for the crust.
2. Add the cold cubed butter to the flour mixture. Use a pastry cutter or your fingers to mix until the mixture resembles coarse crumbs.
3. Gradually add the ice water, 1 tablespoon at a time, mixing with a fork until the dough just comes together.
4. Divide the dough into two equal portions, shape each portion into a disk, wrap them in plastic wrap, and refrigerate for at least 30 minutes before using.

For the Apple Filling:

1. In a large mixing bowl, combine the thinly sliced apples, granulated sugar, brown sugar, flour, ground cinnamon, ground nutmeg, and lemon juice. Toss until the apples are evenly coated with the sugar mixture.

For Assembly:

1. Preheat your oven to 375°F (190°C).
2. Roll out one disk of the chilled pie dough on a lightly floured surface into a circle large enough to fit the bottom and sides of a 9-inch pie dish. Transfer the dough to the pie dish, gently pressing it into the bottom and up the sides.
3. Spoon the apple filling into the prepared pie crust, mounding it slightly in the center. Dot the top of the filling with small pieces of unsalted butter.
4. Roll out the second disk of chilled pie dough on a lightly floured surface into a circle large enough to cover the pie. Carefully place it over the apple filling, sealing the edges with the bottom crust. Trim any excess dough and crimp the edges with a fork or your fingers to seal.
5. Cut slits in the top crust to allow steam to escape during baking.
6. Brush the top crust with the beaten egg and sprinkle with granulated sugar.
7. Place the pie on a baking sheet to catch any drips and transfer it to the preheated oven.
8. Bake for 45-55 minutes, or until the crust is golden brown and the filling is bubbling.
9. If the edges of the crust start to brown too quickly, cover them loosely with aluminum foil.
10. Remove the pie from the oven and let it cool on a wire rack for at least 1 hour before slicing and serving.

Enjoy your delicious classic apple pie, served warm with a scoop of vanilla ice cream or a dollop of whipped cream for an extra special treat!

Peach Cobbler

Ingredients:

For the Peach Filling:

- 6-7 large ripe peaches, peeled, pitted, and sliced
- 1/2 cup granulated sugar
- 1/4 cup packed light brown sugar
- 1 tablespoon lemon juice
- 1 teaspoon vanilla extract
- 1/2 teaspoon ground cinnamon
- 1/4 teaspoon ground nutmeg
- 2 tablespoons cornstarch

For the Cobbler Topping:

- 1 cup all-purpose flour
- 1/2 cup granulated sugar
- 1 teaspoon baking powder
- 1/4 teaspoon salt
- 1/2 cup unsalted butter, melted
- 1/4 cup milk
- Vanilla ice cream or whipped cream, for serving (optional)

Instructions:

1. Preheat your oven to 375°F (190°C).
2. In a large mixing bowl, combine the sliced peaches, granulated sugar, brown sugar, lemon juice, vanilla extract, ground cinnamon, ground nutmeg, and cornstarch. Toss until the peaches are evenly coated with the sugar mixture.
3. Transfer the peach filling to a 9x13-inch baking dish or a similar-sized cast iron skillet, spreading it out evenly.
4. In another mixing bowl, whisk together the flour, granulated sugar, baking powder, and salt for the cobbler topping.
5. Pour the melted butter and milk into the flour mixture. Stir until just combined; the batter will be thick.
6. Drop spoonfuls of the cobbler topping over the peach filling in the baking dish or skillet, spreading it out as evenly as possible.
7. Bake in the preheated oven for 35-40 minutes, or until the cobbler topping is golden brown and the peach filling is bubbling around the edges.
8. Remove the peach cobbler from the oven and let it cool for a few minutes before serving.
9. Serve the peach cobbler warm, with vanilla ice cream or whipped cream if desired.

Enjoy your delicious peach cobbler, with its tender peaches and buttery cobbler topping, for a delightful dessert that's perfect for any occasion!

Blueberry Crisp

Ingredients:

For the Blueberry Filling:

- 6 cups fresh blueberries
- 1/2 cup granulated sugar
- 1 tablespoon lemon juice
- 1 tablespoon cornstarch
- 1 teaspoon vanilla extract
- 1/2 teaspoon ground cinnamon

For the Crisp Topping:

- 1 cup old-fashioned rolled oats
- 1/2 cup all-purpose flour
- 1/2 cup packed light brown sugar
- 1/4 teaspoon salt
- 1/2 cup unsalted butter, cold and cut into small pieces

Instructions:

1. Preheat your oven to 350°F (175°C).
2. In a large mixing bowl, combine the fresh blueberries, granulated sugar, lemon juice, cornstarch, vanilla extract, and ground cinnamon. Toss until the blueberries are evenly coated with the sugar mixture.
3. Transfer the blueberry filling to a 9x9-inch baking dish or a similar-sized cast iron skillet, spreading it out evenly.
4. In another mixing bowl, combine the rolled oats, flour, brown sugar, and salt for the crisp topping.
5. Add the cold, cubed butter to the oat mixture. Use a pastry cutter or your fingers to mix until the mixture resembles coarse crumbs and the butter is evenly distributed.
6. Sprinkle the crisp topping evenly over the blueberry filling in the baking dish or skillet.
7. Bake in the preheated oven for 35-40 minutes, or until the blueberry filling is bubbling and the crisp topping is golden brown and crisp.
8. Remove the blueberry crisp from the oven and let it cool for a few minutes before serving.
9. Serve the blueberry crisp warm, with vanilla ice cream or whipped cream if desired.

Enjoy your delicious blueberry crisp, with its juicy blueberry filling and crunchy oat topping, for a delightful dessert that's perfect for any occasion!

Strawberry Shortcake

Ingredients:

For the Shortcakes:

- 2 cups all-purpose flour
- 1/4 cup granulated sugar
- 1 tablespoon baking powder
- 1/2 teaspoon salt
- 1/2 cup unsalted butter, cold and cut into small pieces
- 2/3 cup milk
- 1 teaspoon vanilla extract

For the Strawberry Filling:

- 4 cups fresh strawberries, hulled and sliced
- 1/4 cup granulated sugar (adjust according to the sweetness of the strawberries)
- 1 tablespoon lemon juice

For Assembly:

- Whipped cream, for serving

Instructions:

For the Shortcakes:

1. Preheat your oven to 425°F (220°C).
2. In a large mixing bowl, whisk together the flour, granulated sugar, baking powder, and salt.
3. Add the cold, cubed butter to the flour mixture. Use a pastry cutter or your fingers to mix until the mixture resembles coarse crumbs and the butter is evenly distributed.
4. In a separate small bowl, combine the milk and vanilla extract.
5. Gradually pour the milk mixture into the flour mixture, stirring until a dough forms.
6. Turn the dough out onto a lightly floured surface and knead it gently a few times until it comes together.
7. Pat the dough out to about 3/4-inch thickness. Use a round cookie cutter or a glass to cut out circles of dough.
8. Place the dough circles on a baking sheet lined with parchment paper, spacing them a few inches apart.
9. Bake in the preheated oven for 12-15 minutes, or until the shortcakes are golden brown and cooked through.
10. Remove the shortcakes from the oven and let them cool on a wire rack.

For the Strawberry Filling:

1. In a mixing bowl, combine the sliced strawberries, granulated sugar, and lemon juice. Toss until the strawberries are evenly coated with the sugar mixture.
2. Let the strawberry mixture sit for about 15-20 minutes to allow the strawberries to release their juices.

For Assembly:

1. To assemble the strawberry shortcakes, slice each cooled shortcake in half horizontally.
2. Place a generous spoonful of the strawberry filling on the bottom half of each shortcake.
3. Top the strawberry filling with a dollop of whipped cream.
4. Place the top half of the shortcake over the whipped cream.
5. Garnish with additional whipped cream and a strawberry slice, if desired.
6. Serve the strawberry shortcakes immediately and enjoy!

This classic dessert is best enjoyed fresh, with tender shortcakes, juicy strawberries, and fluffy whipped cream coming together for a delightful treat!

Raspberry Tart

Ingredients:

For the Tart Crust:

- 1 1/4 cups all-purpose flour
- 1/4 cup granulated sugar
- 1/2 cup unsalted butter, cold and cut into small pieces
- 1 large egg yolk
- 2-3 tablespoons ice water

For the Raspberry Filling:

- 3 cups fresh raspberries
- 1/4 cup granulated sugar (adjust according to the sweetness of the raspberries)
- 2 tablespoons cornstarch
- 1 tablespoon lemon juice
- 1 teaspoon vanilla extract

For Assembly:

- Powdered sugar, for dusting (optional)

Instructions:

For the Tart Crust:

1. In a food processor, combine the flour and granulated sugar. Pulse to mix.
2. Add the cold, cubed butter to the flour mixture. Pulse until the mixture resembles coarse crumbs.
3. Add the egg yolk and 2 tablespoons of ice water to the mixture. Pulse until the dough comes together. If the dough is too dry, add another tablespoon of ice water.
4. Turn the dough out onto a lightly floured surface and shape it into a disk. Wrap the disk in plastic wrap and refrigerate for at least 30 minutes.

For the Raspberry Filling:

1. In a mixing bowl, gently toss together the fresh raspberries, granulated sugar, cornstarch, lemon juice, and vanilla extract until the raspberries are evenly coated.

For Assembly:

1. Preheat your oven to 375°F (190°C).
2. On a lightly floured surface, roll out the chilled tart dough into a circle large enough to fit into a 9-inch tart pan.

3. Carefully transfer the rolled-out dough to the tart pan, pressing it into the bottom and up the sides. Trim any excess dough.
4. Prick the bottom of the tart shell with a fork to prevent it from puffing up during baking.
5. Spread the raspberry filling evenly over the bottom of the tart shell.
6. Place the tart pan on a baking sheet and bake in the preheated oven for 30-35 minutes, or until the crust is golden brown and the filling is bubbly.
7. Remove the raspberry tart from the oven and let it cool completely on a wire rack.
8. Once cooled, dust the top of the tart with powdered sugar, if desired.
9. Slice and serve the raspberry tart, and enjoy!

This raspberry tart is perfect for any occasion, with its buttery crust and vibrant raspberry filling creating a delightful dessert that's sure to impress!

Pineapple Upside-Down Cake

Ingredients:

For the Topping:

- 1/4 cup unsalted butter
- 1/2 cup packed light brown sugar
- 1 can (20 ounces) pineapple slices in juice, drained (reserve the juice)
- Maraschino cherries, drained

For the Cake Batter:

- 1 1/2 cups all-purpose flour
- 1 teaspoon baking powder
- 1/4 teaspoon baking soda
- 1/4 teaspoon salt
- 1/2 cup unsalted butter, softened
- 3/4 cup granulated sugar
- 2 large eggs
- 1 teaspoon vanilla extract
- 1/2 cup reserved pineapple juice
- 1/4 cup buttermilk (or substitute with milk mixed with 1 teaspoon lemon juice or vinegar)

Instructions:

1. Preheat your oven to 350°F (175°C).
2. In a 9-inch round cake pan or cast iron skillet, melt the 1/4 cup of unsalted butter over low heat. Once melted, remove from heat and sprinkle the brown sugar evenly over the melted butter.
3. Arrange the drained pineapple slices on top of the brown sugar mixture, placing a maraschino cherry in the center of each pineapple slice.
4. In a mixing bowl, whisk together the flour, baking powder, baking soda, and salt.
5. In a separate mixing bowl, cream together the softened butter and granulated sugar until light and fluffy.
6. Beat in the eggs, one at a time, followed by the vanilla extract.
7. Gradually add the dry ingredients to the wet ingredients, alternating with the reserved pineapple juice and buttermilk, beginning and ending with the dry ingredients. Mix until just combined.
8. Pour the cake batter over the pineapple slices in the cake pan or skillet, spreading it out evenly.
9. Bake in the preheated oven for 40-45 minutes, or until a toothpick inserted into the center of the cake comes out clean.
10. Remove the cake from the oven and let it cool in the pan or skillet for 5 minutes.

11. Place a serving platter upside-down on top of the cake pan or skillet, then carefully invert the cake onto the platter. Carefully lift off the pan or skillet.
12. Allow the cake to cool slightly before slicing and serving.

Enjoy your delicious pineapple upside-down cake, with its caramelized pineapple and cherry topping and moist cake, for a classic and nostalgic dessert!

Mango Sorbet

Ingredients:

- 4 ripe mangoes, peeled, pitted, and diced
- 1/2 cup granulated sugar (adjust according to the sweetness of the mangoes)
- 1/4 cup water
- 2 tablespoons fresh lime juice
- Optional: Fresh mint leaves or lime zest for garnish

Instructions:

1. In a small saucepan, combine the granulated sugar and water. Heat over medium heat, stirring occasionally, until the sugar has completely dissolved to make a simple syrup. Remove from heat and let it cool completely.
2. Place the diced mangoes in a blender or food processor. Add the cooled simple syrup and fresh lime juice.
3. Blend the mixture until smooth and creamy.
4. If desired, strain the mango puree through a fine-mesh sieve to remove any fibrous bits.
5. Transfer the mango puree to a shallow dish or baking pan. Cover with plastic wrap and place it in the freezer.
6. Every 30 minutes, use a fork to scrape and stir the partially frozen sorbet mixture to break up any ice crystals and achieve a smooth texture.
7. Continue this process until the sorbet is completely frozen and has a smooth consistency, which will take about 3-4 hours.
8. Once the sorbet is frozen, scoop it into bowls or glasses to serve.
9. Garnish with fresh mint leaves or lime zest, if desired.

Enjoy your refreshing mango sorbet on its own or as a palate cleanser between courses. It's the perfect treat for hot summer days or any time you're craving a tropical indulgence!

Kiwi Lime Pie

Ingredients:

For the Crust:

- 1 1/2 cups graham cracker crumbs
- 1/4 cup granulated sugar
- 1/2 cup unsalted butter, melted

For the Filling:

- 4-5 large kiwifruits, peeled and sliced
- 1/2 cup fresh lime juice (about 4-5 limes)
- 1 tablespoon lime zest
- 1 can (14 ounces) sweetened condensed milk
- 4 large egg yolks

For Garnish (optional):

- Whipped cream
- Slices of kiwifruit
- Lime zest

Instructions:

For the Crust:

1. Preheat your oven to 350°F (175°C).
2. In a mixing bowl, combine the graham cracker crumbs, granulated sugar, and melted butter. Stir until the mixture resembles wet sand.
3. Press the mixture into the bottom and up the sides of a 9-inch pie dish, forming an even crust.
4. Bake the crust in the preheated oven for 8-10 minutes, or until lightly golden brown. Remove from the oven and let it cool completely.

For the Filling:

1. In a blender or food processor, combine the sliced kiwifruits, lime juice, and lime zest. Blend until smooth.
2. In a separate mixing bowl, whisk together the sweetened condensed milk and egg yolks until well combined.
3. Gradually add the kiwi-lime mixture to the condensed milk mixture, whisking until smooth and well incorporated.
4. Pour the filling into the cooled graham cracker crust, spreading it out evenly.

5. Bake the pie in the preheated oven for 15-20 minutes, or until the filling is set and slightly firm to the touch.
6. Remove the pie from the oven and let it cool to room temperature.
7. Once cooled, refrigerate the pie for at least 2-3 hours, or until chilled and set.

For Garnish (optional):

1. Before serving, garnish the chilled pie with whipped cream, slices of kiwifruit, and lime zest, if desired.
2. Slice and serve the kiwi lime pie, and enjoy its refreshing and tangy flavor!

This kiwi lime pie is a delightful twist on the classic key lime pie, with the tropical flavor of kiwifruit adding a unique and refreshing touch. It's perfect for serving at summer gatherings or as a light and refreshing dessert any time of the year!

Grapefruit Bars

Ingredients:

For the Crust:

- 1 cup all-purpose flour
- 1/4 cup granulated sugar
- 1/2 cup unsalted butter, softened

For the Filling:

- 1 cup granulated sugar
- 3 large eggs
- 1/3 cup freshly squeezed grapefruit juice
- 2 tablespoons grapefruit zest
- 2 tablespoons all-purpose flour
- 1/2 teaspoon baking powder
- Powdered sugar, for dusting

Instructions:

For the Crust:

1. Preheat your oven to 350°F (175°C). Grease or line an 8x8-inch baking dish with parchment paper, leaving an overhang on the sides for easy removal.
2. In a mixing bowl, combine the all-purpose flour, granulated sugar, and softened butter. Mix until the mixture resembles coarse crumbs.
3. Press the mixture evenly into the bottom of the prepared baking dish.
4. Bake the crust in the preheated oven for 15-18 minutes, or until lightly golden brown.

For the Filling:

1. In a separate mixing bowl, whisk together the granulated sugar, eggs, grapefruit juice, and grapefruit zest until well combined.
2. In another bowl, sift together the all-purpose flour and baking powder.
3. Gradually add the flour mixture to the wet ingredients, whisking until smooth and no lumps remain.
4. Pour the filling over the partially baked crust.
5. Return the baking dish to the oven and bake for an additional 20-25 minutes, or until the filling is set and the edges are lightly golden brown.
6. Remove the baking dish from the oven and let it cool completely on a wire rack.
7. Once cooled, refrigerate the grapefruit bars for at least 1-2 hours to chill and set.
8. Once chilled, use the parchment paper overhang to lift the bars out of the baking dish. Place them on a cutting board and cut into squares or bars.

9. Dust the tops of the grapefruit bars with powdered sugar before serving.

Enjoy your tangy and refreshing grapefruit bars as a delightful citrusy treat! They're perfect for serving at brunches, picnics, or as a light and refreshing dessert any time of the year.

Watermelon Granita

Ingredients:

- 4 cups seedless watermelon, cubed
- 1/4 cup granulated sugar (adjust according to the sweetness of the watermelon)
- 2 tablespoons freshly squeezed lime juice
- Mint leaves, for garnish (optional)

Instructions:

1. Place the cubed watermelon in a blender or food processor. Blend until smooth.
2. Strain the watermelon puree through a fine-mesh sieve into a shallow baking dish to remove any seeds or pulp.
3. Stir in the granulated sugar and lime juice until the sugar has dissolved.
4. Place the baking dish in the freezer and let it freeze for about 1 hour.
5. After 1 hour, use a fork to scrape and stir the partially frozen granita, breaking up any ice crystals that have formed.
6. Return the baking dish to the freezer and continue to freeze for another 2-3 hours, scraping and stirring the mixture every 30 minutes, until the granita is fully frozen and has a light, fluffy texture.
7. Once the granita is frozen, use a fork to scrape the mixture into icy flakes.
8. Scoop the watermelon granita into serving glasses or bowls.
9. Garnish with fresh mint leaves, if desired.
10. Serve immediately and enjoy the refreshing taste of watermelon granita!

This watermelon granita is a simple and delicious way to enjoy the natural sweetness of watermelon. It's perfect for cooling down on hot summer days and makes a light and refreshing dessert for any occasion.

Lemon Meringue Pie

Ingredients:

For the Pie Crust:

- 1 1/4 cups all-purpose flour
- 1/2 teaspoon salt
- 1/2 cup unsalted butter, cold and cubed
- 3-4 tablespoons ice water

For the Lemon Filling:

- 1 cup granulated sugar
- 1/4 cup cornstarch
- 1/4 teaspoon salt
- 1 1/2 cups water
- 4 large egg yolks
- 1 tablespoon lemon zest
- 1/2 cup freshly squeezed lemon juice
- 2 tablespoons unsalted butter

For the Meringue:

- 4 large egg whites, at room temperature
- 1/2 cup granulated sugar
- 1/4 teaspoon cream of tartar

Instructions:

For the Pie Crust:

1. In a large mixing bowl, whisk together the flour and salt.
2. Add the cold, cubed butter to the flour mixture. Use a pastry cutter or your fingers to mix until the mixture resembles coarse crumbs.
3. Gradually add the ice water, 1 tablespoon at a time, mixing with a fork until the dough just comes together.
4. Shape the dough into a disk, wrap it in plastic wrap, and refrigerate for at least 30 minutes before using.
5. Preheat your oven to 375°F (190°C).
6. On a lightly floured surface, roll out the chilled pie dough into a circle large enough to fit into a 9-inch pie dish. Transfer the dough to the pie dish, gently pressing it into the bottom and up the sides. Trim any excess dough and crimp the edges. Prick the bottom of the crust with a fork.

7. Line the crust with parchment paper or aluminum foil and fill it with pie weights or dried beans. Bake in the preheated oven for 15 minutes. Remove the weights and parchment paper, and bake for an additional 10-12 minutes, or until the crust is golden brown. Remove from the oven and let it cool completely.

For the Lemon Filling:

1. In a medium saucepan, whisk together the granulated sugar, cornstarch, and salt.
2. Gradually whisk in the water until smooth.
3. Place the saucepan over medium heat and cook, stirring constantly, until the mixture thickens and comes to a boil.
4. Boil for 1 minute, then remove the saucepan from the heat.
5. In a separate mixing bowl, whisk the egg yolks until smooth. Gradually whisk in about 1/2 cup of the hot sugar mixture to temper the eggs.
6. Pour the tempered egg mixture back into the saucepan with the remaining sugar mixture, whisking constantly.
7. Return the saucepan to medium heat and cook, stirring constantly, for an additional 2-3 minutes, or until thickened.
8. Remove the saucepan from the heat and stir in the lemon zest, lemon juice, and butter until smooth.
9. Pour the lemon filling into the cooled pie crust, spreading it out evenly. Set aside while you make the meringue.

For the Meringue:

1. Preheat your oven to 350°F (175°C).
2. In a clean mixing bowl, beat the egg whites with an electric mixer on medium speed until foamy.
3. Add the cream of tartar and continue to beat until soft peaks form.
4. Gradually add the granulated sugar, 1 tablespoon at a time, while continuing to beat on high speed until stiff, glossy peaks form.
5. Spread the meringue over the lemon filling in the pie dish, making sure to spread it all the way to the edges to seal in the filling.
6. Use the back of a spoon to create peaks in the meringue.
7. Bake the pie in the preheated oven for 10-12 minutes, or until the meringue is lightly golden brown.
8. Remove the pie from the oven and let it cool completely on a wire rack.
9. Once cooled, refrigerate the pie for at least 2-3 hours before serving to allow the filling to set.
10. Slice and serve the lemon meringue pie, and enjoy!

This classic lemon meringue pie is sure to impress with its tangy lemon filling and fluffy meringue topping. It's perfect for any occasion and guaranteed to be a crowd-pleaser!

Blackberry Crumble

Ingredients:

For the Blackberry Filling:

- 4 cups fresh blackberries
- 1/2 cup granulated sugar (adjust according to the sweetness of the blackberries)
- 2 tablespoons cornstarch
- 1 tablespoon freshly squeezed lemon juice
- 1 teaspoon lemon zest (optional)

For the Crumble Topping:

- 1 cup old-fashioned rolled oats
- 1/2 cup all-purpose flour
- 1/2 cup packed light brown sugar
- 1/4 teaspoon salt
- 1/2 cup unsalted butter, melted

Instructions:

1. Preheat your oven to 350°F (175°C). Grease a 9x9-inch baking dish or a similar-sized cast iron skillet.
2. In a large mixing bowl, combine the blackberries, granulated sugar, cornstarch, lemon juice, and lemon zest (if using). Toss until the blackberries are evenly coated with the sugar mixture.
3. Transfer the blackberry filling to the prepared baking dish or skillet, spreading it out evenly.
4. In another mixing bowl, combine the rolled oats, flour, brown sugar, and salt for the crumble topping.
5. Pour the melted butter over the oat mixture and stir until well combined and crumbly.
6. Sprinkle the crumble topping evenly over the blackberry filling in the baking dish or skillet.
7. Bake in the preheated oven for 35-40 minutes, or until the blackberry filling is bubbling and the crumble topping is golden brown and crisp.
8. Remove the blackberry crumble from the oven and let it cool for a few minutes before serving.
9. Serve the blackberry crumble warm, with a scoop of vanilla ice cream or a dollop of whipped cream if desired.

Enjoy your delicious blackberry crumble, with its juicy blackberry filling and crunchy oat topping, for a delightful dessert that's perfect for any occasion!

Cherry Clafoutis

Ingredients:

- 1 tablespoon unsalted butter, for greasing the baking dish
- 1 cup fresh cherries, pitted
- 2/3 cup granulated sugar, divided
- 3 large eggs
- 1 cup whole milk
- 1/2 cup all-purpose flour
- 1 teaspoon vanilla extract
- 1/4 teaspoon almond extract (optional)
- Powdered sugar, for dusting

Instructions:

1. Preheat your oven to 350°F (175°C). Grease a 9-inch round baking dish with the unsalted butter.
2. Arrange the pitted cherries in a single layer in the bottom of the greased baking dish. Sprinkle 1/3 cup of the granulated sugar over the cherries.
3. In a mixing bowl, whisk together the eggs, remaining 1/3 cup of granulated sugar, whole milk, all-purpose flour, vanilla extract, and almond extract (if using) until smooth.
4. Pour the batter evenly over the cherries in the baking dish.
5. Bake in the preheated oven for 35-40 minutes, or until the clafoutis is set and golden brown on top.
6. Remove the clafoutis from the oven and let it cool for a few minutes.
7. Dust the top of the clafoutis with powdered sugar.
8. Slice and serve the cherry clafoutis warm or at room temperature.

Enjoy your delicious cherry clafoutis, with its tender cherries and custardy texture, for a delightful dessert that's perfect for any occasion!

Pear Frangipane Tart

Ingredients:

For the Pastry Crust:

- 1 1/4 cups all-purpose flour
- 1/4 cup granulated sugar
- 1/4 teaspoon salt
- 1/2 cup unsalted butter, cold and cut into small pieces
- 1 large egg yolk
- 1-2 tablespoons ice water

For the Frangipane Filling:

- 1/2 cup unsalted butter, softened
- 1/2 cup granulated sugar
- 1 large egg
- 1 cup almond flour
- 1 tablespoon all-purpose flour
- 1 teaspoon vanilla extract

For Assembly:

- 2-3 ripe pears, peeled, cored, and thinly sliced
- 2 tablespoons apricot preserves or fruit jam (optional, for glazing)

Instructions:

For the Pastry Crust:

1. In a food processor, combine the all-purpose flour, granulated sugar, and salt. Pulse to mix.
2. Add the cold, cubed butter to the flour mixture. Pulse until the mixture resembles coarse crumbs.
3. Add the egg yolk and 1 tablespoon of ice water to the mixture. Pulse until the dough starts to come together. If needed, add an additional tablespoon of ice water.
4. Turn the dough out onto a lightly floured surface and shape it into a disk. Wrap the disk in plastic wrap and refrigerate for at least 30 minutes.
5. Preheat your oven to 375°F (190°C). Roll out the chilled dough on a lightly floured surface to fit into a 9-inch tart pan with a removable bottom. Press the dough into the pan, trimming any excess. Prick the bottom of the crust with a fork. Line the crust with parchment paper or aluminum foil and fill it with pie weights or dried beans.

6. Bake the crust in the preheated oven for 15 minutes. Remove the weights and parchment paper or foil, and bake for an additional 5-7 minutes, or until lightly golden brown. Remove from the oven and let it cool slightly.

For the Frangipane Filling:

1. In a mixing bowl, cream together the softened butter and granulated sugar until light and fluffy.
2. Beat in the egg until well combined.
3. Stir in the almond flour, all-purpose flour, and vanilla extract until smooth and creamy.

For Assembly:

1. Spread the frangipane filling evenly over the cooled pastry crust.
2. Arrange the sliced pears on top of the frangipane in an attractive pattern.
3. If desired, heat the apricot preserves or fruit jam in a small saucepan over low heat until melted. Brush the melted preserves or jam over the top of the pears for a shiny glaze.
4. Bake the tart in the preheated oven for 30-35 minutes, or until the frangipane is set and golden brown.
5. Remove the tart from the oven and let it cool slightly before slicing and serving.

Enjoy your delicious pear frangipane tart, with its tender pears and almond filling, for a delightful dessert that's perfect for any occasion!

Plum Galette

Ingredients:

For the Pastry Crust:

- 1 1/4 cups all-purpose flour
- 1/2 teaspoon granulated sugar
- 1/4 teaspoon salt
- 1/2 cup unsalted butter, cold and cut into small pieces
- 3-4 tablespoons ice water

For the Plum Filling:

- 4-5 ripe plums, pitted and sliced
- 1/4 cup granulated sugar
- 1 tablespoon cornstarch
- 1 tablespoon lemon juice
- 1/2 teaspoon ground cinnamon (optional)

For Assembly:

- 1 tablespoon unsalted butter, cut into small pieces
- 1 tablespoon milk or cream (for brushing the pastry)
- 1 tablespoon granulated sugar (for sprinkling)
- Vanilla ice cream or whipped cream, for serving (optional)

Instructions:

For the Pastry Crust:

1. In a food processor, combine the all-purpose flour, granulated sugar, and salt. Pulse to mix.
2. Add the cold, cubed butter to the flour mixture. Pulse until the mixture resembles coarse crumbs.
3. Gradually add the ice water, 1 tablespoon at a time, pulsing until the dough starts to come together. Add only as much water as needed.
4. Turn the dough out onto a lightly floured surface and shape it into a disk. Wrap the disk in plastic wrap and refrigerate for at least 30 minutes.

For the Plum Filling:

1. In a mixing bowl, combine the sliced plums, granulated sugar, cornstarch, lemon juice, and ground cinnamon (if using). Toss until the plums are evenly coated.

For Assembly:

1. Preheat your oven to 375°F (190°C). Line a baking sheet with parchment paper.
2. On a lightly floured surface, roll out the chilled pastry dough into a circle about 12 inches in diameter and 1/8 inch thick.
3. Carefully transfer the rolled-out dough to the prepared baking sheet.
4. Arrange the plum slices in the center of the dough, leaving a border of about 2 inches around the edges.
5. Fold the edges of the dough over the plum filling, pleating as necessary.
6. Dot the plum filling with small pieces of unsalted butter.
7. Brush the edges of the pastry with milk or cream and sprinkle with granulated sugar.
8. Bake the galette in the preheated oven for 30-35 minutes, or until the crust is golden brown and the plum filling is bubbling.
9. Remove the galette from the oven and let it cool slightly before serving.
10. Serve slices of the plum galette warm or at room temperature, with vanilla ice cream or whipped cream if desired.

Enjoy your delicious plum galette, with its tender fruit filling and flaky pastry crust, for a delightful dessert that's perfect for any occasion!

Banana Bread

Ingredients:

- 2 to 3 ripe bananas, mashed (about 1 cup)
- 1/3 cup unsalted butter, melted
- 1/2 cup granulated sugar
- 1/4 cup packed light brown sugar
- 1 large egg, beaten
- 1 teaspoon vanilla extract
- 1 teaspoon baking soda
- Pinch of salt
- 1 1/2 cups all-purpose flour

Optional Add-ins:

- 1/2 cup chopped nuts (such as walnuts or pecans)
- 1/2 cup chocolate chips
- 1/2 cup dried fruit (such as raisins or cranberries)

Instructions:

1. Preheat your oven to 350°F (175°C). Grease a 9x5-inch loaf pan or line it with parchment paper.
2. In a mixing bowl, mash the ripe bananas with a fork or potato masher until smooth.
3. Stir in the melted butter.
4. Add the granulated sugar, brown sugar, beaten egg, and vanilla extract to the banana mixture. Mix until well combined.
5. Sprinkle the baking soda and salt over the mixture, and stir to incorporate.
6. Gradually add the all-purpose flour to the wet ingredients, mixing until just combined. Be careful not to overmix.
7. If using any add-ins (nuts, chocolate chips, or dried fruit), fold them into the batter until evenly distributed.
8. Pour the batter into the prepared loaf pan, spreading it out evenly.
9. Bake in the preheated oven for 50 to 60 minutes, or until a toothpick inserted into the center comes out clean.
10. If the top of the banana bread starts to brown too quickly, you can tent it loosely with aluminum foil during the last 15-20 minutes of baking.
11. Once baked, remove the banana bread from the oven and let it cool in the pan for 10 minutes.
12. After 10 minutes, remove the banana bread from the pan and transfer it to a wire rack to cool completely before slicing and serving.

Enjoy your homemade banana bread warm or at room temperature, with a pat of butter, a drizzle of honey, or simply on its own. It's perfect for breakfast, as a snack, or as a comforting treat any time of the day!

Coconut Macaroons with Pineapple

Ingredients:

- 3 cups sweetened shredded coconut
- 1 cup finely chopped pineapple (fresh or canned, drained well)
- 1/2 cup granulated sugar
- 2 large egg whites
- 1 teaspoon vanilla extract
- 1/4 teaspoon salt

Instructions:

1. Preheat your oven to 325°F (160°C). Line a baking sheet with parchment paper.
2. In a large mixing bowl, combine the sweetened shredded coconut, finely chopped pineapple, granulated sugar, vanilla extract, and salt. Mix until well combined.
3. In a separate mixing bowl, beat the egg whites until stiff peaks form.
4. Gently fold the beaten egg whites into the coconut-pineapple mixture until evenly combined.
5. Using a spoon or cookie scoop, drop rounded tablespoons of the mixture onto the prepared baking sheet, spacing them about 1 inch apart.
6. Bake in the preheated oven for 20-25 minutes, or until the macaroons are lightly golden brown on the outside.
7. Remove the baking sheet from the oven and let the macaroons cool on the pan for a few minutes before transferring them to a wire rack to cool completely.

Enjoy your delicious coconut macaroons with pineapple! They're perfect for serving as a sweet treat or dessert, and the tropical flavor adds a delightful twist to the classic coconut macaroon recipe.

Orange Almond Cake

Ingredients:

For the Cake:

- 1 cup almond flour
- 1 cup all-purpose flour
- 1 cup granulated sugar
- 1 teaspoon baking powder
- 1/4 teaspoon salt
- 3 large eggs
- 1/2 cup unsalted butter, melted
- 1/4 cup freshly squeezed orange juice
- 1 tablespoon orange zest
- 1 teaspoon vanilla extract

For the Glaze (optional):

- 1 cup powdered sugar
- 2-3 tablespoons freshly squeezed orange juice
- 1 teaspoon orange zest

Instructions:

1. Preheat your oven to 350°F (175°C). Grease a 9-inch round cake pan and line the bottom with parchment paper.
2. In a mixing bowl, whisk together the almond flour, all-purpose flour, granulated sugar, baking powder, and salt until well combined.
3. In a separate mixing bowl, beat the eggs until light and frothy.
4. Add the melted butter, orange juice, orange zest, and vanilla extract to the beaten eggs. Mix until well combined.
5. Gradually add the dry ingredients to the wet ingredients, mixing until just combined. Be careful not to overmix.
6. Pour the batter into the prepared cake pan and spread it out evenly.
7. Bake in the preheated oven for 30-35 minutes, or until a toothpick inserted into the center comes out clean.
8. Remove the cake from the oven and let it cool in the pan for 10 minutes before transferring it to a wire rack to cool completely.

For the Glaze (optional):

1. In a small mixing bowl, whisk together the powdered sugar, freshly squeezed orange juice, and orange zest until smooth and well combined.
2. Once the cake has cooled completely, drizzle the glaze over the top of the cake.

3. Allow the glaze to set for a few minutes before slicing and serving.

Enjoy your delicious orange almond cake! It's perfect for serving as a dessert or for enjoying with a cup of tea or coffee. The combination of orange and almond flavors makes for a delightful treat that's sure to please.

Fig and Honey Cheesecake

Ingredients:

For the Crust:

- 1 1/2 cups graham cracker crumbs
- 1/4 cup granulated sugar
- 1/2 cup unsalted butter, melted

For the Cheesecake Filling:

- 24 oz (three 8-ounce packages) cream cheese, softened
- 3/4 cup granulated sugar
- 3 large eggs
- 1 teaspoon vanilla extract
- 1/4 cup honey
- 1/4 cup heavy cream
- 1/2 cup fig preserves or jam

For the Topping:

- Fresh figs, sliced (optional)
- Honey, for drizzling

Instructions:

For the Crust:

1. Preheat your oven to 325°F (160°C). Grease a 9-inch springform pan.
2. In a mixing bowl, combine the graham cracker crumbs, granulated sugar, and melted butter. Mix until well combined.
3. Press the mixture into the bottom of the prepared springform pan, using the back of a spoon or your fingers to pack it down evenly.
4. Bake the crust in the preheated oven for 10 minutes. Remove from the oven and let it cool while you prepare the filling.

For the Cheesecake Filling:

1. In a large mixing bowl, beat the softened cream cheese and granulated sugar until smooth and creamy.
2. Add the eggs, one at a time, beating well after each addition.
3. Stir in the vanilla extract, honey, and heavy cream until well combined.
4. Pour the cheesecake filling over the cooled crust in the springform pan.
5. Drop spoonfuls of fig preserves or jam onto the surface of the cheesecake filling.

6. Use a knife or toothpick to gently swirl the fig preserves or jam into the cheesecake filling, creating a marbled effect.
7. Bake the cheesecake in the preheated oven for 45-50 minutes, or until the edges are set but the center still jiggles slightly.
8. Turn off the oven and leave the cheesecake in the oven with the door closed for 1 hour to cool gradually.
9. Remove the cheesecake from the oven and let it cool completely on a wire rack.
10. Once cooled, refrigerate the cheesecake for at least 4 hours, or preferably overnight, to chill and set.

For Serving:

1. Before serving, carefully run a knife around the edge of the springform pan to loosen the cheesecake.
2. Remove the sides of the springform pan.
3. Garnish the top of the cheesecake with fresh fig slices, if desired, and drizzle with honey.
4. Slice and serve the fig and honey cheesecake, and enjoy!

This fig and honey cheesecake is a decadent and elegant dessert that's perfect for special occasions or anytime you want to indulge in a luxurious treat. The combination of creamy cheesecake, sweet figs, and fragrant honey creates a delightful flavor profile that's sure to impress!

Cranberry Orange Bread

Ingredients:

- 2 cups all-purpose flour
- 1 cup granulated sugar
- 1 1/2 teaspoons baking powder
- 1/2 teaspoon baking soda
- 1/2 teaspoon salt
- 1 cup fresh cranberries, chopped (or frozen cranberries, thawed)
- 1/3 cup vegetable oil
- 2 large eggs
- 3/4 cup freshly squeezed orange juice
- 1 tablespoon orange zest

Optional Glaze:

- 1 cup powdered sugar
- 2-3 tablespoons freshly squeezed orange juice
- 1 teaspoon orange zest

Instructions:

1. Preheat your oven to 350°F (175°C). Grease a 9x5-inch loaf pan or line it with parchment paper.
2. In a large mixing bowl, whisk together the all-purpose flour, granulated sugar, baking powder, baking soda, and salt until well combined.
3. Gently fold in the chopped cranberries until evenly distributed in the flour mixture.
4. In a separate mixing bowl, whisk together the vegetable oil, eggs, freshly squeezed orange juice, and orange zest until well combined.
5. Gradually add the wet ingredients to the dry ingredients, mixing until just combined. Be careful not to overmix.
6. Pour the batter into the prepared loaf pan, spreading it out evenly.
7. Bake in the preheated oven for 50-60 minutes, or until a toothpick inserted into the center comes out clean.
8. Remove the bread from the oven and let it cool in the pan for 10 minutes before transferring it to a wire rack to cool completely.

Optional Glaze:

1. In a small mixing bowl, whisk together the powdered sugar, freshly squeezed orange juice, and orange zest until smooth and well combined.
2. Once the bread has cooled completely, drizzle the glaze over the top of the bread.
3. Allow the glaze to set for a few minutes before slicing and serving.

Enjoy your delicious cranberry orange bread! It's perfect for enjoying on its own, toasted with butter, or served with a cup of tea or coffee. The tangy cranberries and citrusy orange flavor make for a delightful and refreshing combination.

Mixed Berry Fool

Ingredients:

- 2 cups mixed berries (such as strawberries, raspberries, blueberries, and blackberries), fresh or frozen
- 1/4 cup granulated sugar (adjust according to the sweetness of the berries)
- 1 tablespoon lemon juice
- 1 cup heavy cream
- 1/4 cup powdered sugar
- 1 teaspoon vanilla extract

Optional Garnish:

- Fresh berries, for topping

Instructions:

1. If using frozen berries, thaw them completely before proceeding.
2. In a blender or food processor, puree the mixed berries until smooth.
3. Pour the berry puree into a saucepan and add the granulated sugar and lemon juice. Stir to combine.
4. Cook the berry mixture over medium heat, stirring occasionally, until it thickens slightly and reduces, about 5-7 minutes.
5. Remove the berry mixture from the heat and let it cool completely.
6. In a mixing bowl, whip the heavy cream, powdered sugar, and vanilla extract until stiff peaks form.
7. Gently fold the cooled berry puree into the whipped cream, swirling it to create a marbled effect.
8. Divide the berry fool among serving glasses or bowls.
9. Optional: Garnish the top of each serving with fresh berries.
10. Refrigerate the mixed berry fool for at least 1 hour before serving to allow the flavors to meld.

Enjoy your delicious mixed berry fool! It's a light and refreshing dessert that's perfect for any occasion, and the combination of sweet whipped cream and tangy berry puree is sure to be a crowd-pleaser.

Apple Crisp Bars

Ingredients:

For the Crust and Topping:

- 1 1/2 cups all-purpose flour
- 1 1/2 cups old-fashioned rolled oats
- 1 cup packed light brown sugar
- 1/2 teaspoon baking powder
- 1/2 teaspoon ground cinnamon
- 1/4 teaspoon salt
- 3/4 cup unsalted butter, melted

For the Apple Filling:

- 4 cups peeled, cored, and thinly sliced apples (such as Granny Smith or Honeycrisp)
- 1/4 cup granulated sugar
- 2 tablespoons all-purpose flour
- 1 tablespoon lemon juice
- 1/2 teaspoon ground cinnamon
- 1/4 teaspoon ground nutmeg
- Pinch of salt

Instructions:

1. Preheat your oven to 350°F (175°C). Grease a 9x9-inch baking dish or line it with parchment paper, leaving an overhang on the sides for easy removal.
2. In a large mixing bowl, combine the all-purpose flour, rolled oats, brown sugar, baking powder, ground cinnamon, and salt for the crust and topping.
3. Pour the melted butter over the dry ingredients and stir until well combined and crumbly.
4. Press about two-thirds of the mixture into the bottom of the prepared baking dish to form the crust. Set aside the remaining mixture for the topping.
5. In another mixing bowl, combine the sliced apples, granulated sugar, all-purpose flour, lemon juice, ground cinnamon, ground nutmeg, and salt for the apple filling. Toss until the apples are evenly coated.
6. Spread the apple filling evenly over the crust in the baking dish.
7. Sprinkle the reserved crumb mixture evenly over the apple filling to form the topping.
8. Bake in the preheated oven for 40-45 minutes, or until the topping is golden brown and the apple filling is bubbly.
9. Remove the baking dish from the oven and let the apple crisp bars cool completely on a wire rack.
10. Once cooled, use the parchment paper overhang to lift the bars out of the baking dish. Cut into squares or bars.

11. Serve the apple crisp bars warm or at room temperature. Optionally, you can serve them with a scoop of vanilla ice cream or a dollop of whipped cream.

Enjoy your delicious apple crisp bars, with their buttery oat crust and flavorful apple filling! They're perfect for dessert or as a sweet treat any time of the day.

Grilled Peaches with Honey and Mascarpone

Ingredients:

- 4 ripe but firm peaches, halved and pitted
- 1 tablespoon olive oil or melted butter
- 1/4 cup honey, plus extra for drizzling
- 1/2 cup mascarpone cheese
- Fresh mint leaves, for garnish (optional)

Instructions:

1. Preheat your grill to medium-high heat.
2. Brush the cut sides of the peach halves with olive oil or melted butter to prevent sticking.
3. Place the peach halves, cut side down, on the preheated grill. Grill for 3-4 minutes, or until grill marks form and the peaches are slightly softened.
4. Carefully flip the peach halves over using tongs.
5. Drizzle the grilled side of each peach half with honey. Continue grilling for another 3-4 minutes, or until the peaches are tender and caramelized.
6. Remove the grilled peach halves from the grill and let them cool slightly.
7. To serve, place a grilled peach half on each serving plate. Spoon a dollop of mascarpone cheese onto each peach half.
8. Drizzle additional honey over the top of the mascarpone cheese and grilled peaches.
9. Garnish with fresh mint leaves, if desired, for a pop of color and flavor.
10. Serve the grilled peaches with honey and mascarpone immediately while still warm.

Enjoy your delicious grilled peaches with honey and mascarpone! They make for a delightful and sophisticated dessert that's perfect for summer gatherings or any special occasion.

Strawberry Rhubarb Crisp

Ingredients:

For the Filling:

- 3 cups sliced rhubarb (about 1/2-inch thick)
- 3 cups sliced strawberries
- 1/2 cup granulated sugar
- 1/4 cup all-purpose flour
- 1 tablespoon lemon juice
- 1 teaspoon vanilla extract

For the Crumble Topping:

- 1 cup old-fashioned rolled oats
- 1/2 cup all-purpose flour
- 1/2 cup packed light brown sugar
- 1/2 teaspoon ground cinnamon
- 1/4 teaspoon salt
- 1/2 cup unsalted butter, melted

Instructions:

1. Preheat your oven to 375°F (190°C). Grease a 9x9-inch baking dish or a similar-sized baking dish.
2. In a large mixing bowl, combine the sliced rhubarb, sliced strawberries, granulated sugar, all-purpose flour, lemon juice, and vanilla extract for the filling. Toss until the fruit is evenly coated.
3. In another mixing bowl, combine the old-fashioned rolled oats, all-purpose flour, packed light brown sugar, ground cinnamon, and salt for the crumble topping.
4. Pour the melted unsalted butter over the dry ingredients for the crumble topping. Stir until the mixture resembles coarse crumbs and is evenly moistened.
5. Spread the fruit filling mixture evenly into the prepared baking dish.
6. Sprinkle the crumble topping evenly over the fruit filling, covering it completely.
7. Place the baking dish on a baking sheet to catch any potential drips, and bake in the preheated oven for 35-40 minutes, or until the fruit is bubbly and the topping is golden brown.
8. Remove the strawberry rhubarb crisp from the oven and let it cool for a few minutes before serving.
9. Serve warm, optionally with a scoop of vanilla ice cream or a dollop of whipped cream.

Enjoy your delicious strawberry rhubarb crisp! It's a comforting and irresistible dessert that's perfect for any occasion, especially during rhubarb season.

Pineapple Coconut Tiramisu

Ingredients:

For the Pineapple Coconut Sauce:

- 1 cup crushed pineapple (fresh or canned, drained)
- 1/2 cup coconut milk
- 1/4 cup granulated sugar

For the Tiramisu:

- 1 cup heavy cream
- 8 oz mascarpone cheese, softened
- 1/4 cup powdered sugar
- 1 teaspoon vanilla extract
- 1 1/2 cups shredded coconut, toasted
- 24 ladyfinger cookies
- 1 cup pineapple chunks (fresh or canned, drained)

Instructions:

For the Pineapple Coconut Sauce:

1. In a small saucepan, combine the crushed pineapple, coconut milk, and granulated sugar.
2. Cook over medium heat, stirring occasionally, until the mixture thickens slightly, about 5-7 minutes.
3. Remove from heat and let it cool completely.

For the Tiramisu:

1. In a mixing bowl, beat the heavy cream until stiff peaks form.
2. In another mixing bowl, combine the softened mascarpone cheese, powdered sugar, and vanilla extract. Mix until smooth.
3. Gently fold the whipped cream into the mascarpone mixture until well combined.
4. Spread a thin layer of the pineapple coconut sauce on the bottom of a 9x13-inch baking dish.
5. Dip each ladyfinger cookie into the remaining pineapple coconut sauce, ensuring they are well coated but not overly soaked.
6. Arrange a layer of dipped ladyfinger cookies in the bottom of the baking dish.
7. Spread half of the mascarpone mixture over the layer of ladyfingers.
8. Sprinkle half of the toasted shredded coconut evenly over the mascarpone mixture.
9. Arrange half of the pineapple chunks over the shredded coconut.

10. Repeat the layers with the remaining dipped ladyfinger cookies, mascarpone mixture, shredded coconut, and pineapple chunks.
11. Cover the tiramisu with plastic wrap and refrigerate for at least 4 hours, or preferably overnight, to allow the flavors to meld and the dessert to set.
12. Before serving, garnish the top of the tiramisu with additional toasted shredded coconut and pineapple chunks, if desired.

Enjoy your delicious pineapple coconut tiramisu! It's a refreshing and tropical dessert that's perfect for summer gatherings or any special occasion.

Mango Sticky Rice

Ingredients:

For the Sticky Rice:

- 1 cup glutinous rice (also known as sticky rice or sweet rice)
- 1 cup coconut milk
- 1/4 cup granulated sugar
- 1/4 teaspoon salt

For Serving:

- 2 ripe mangoes, peeled, pitted, and sliced
- Toasted sesame seeds or toasted mung beans (optional, for garnish)
- Extra coconut milk (optional, for drizzling)

Instructions:

1. Rinse the glutinous rice under cold water until the water runs clear. Then, soak the rice in water for at least 4 hours or overnight.
2. After soaking, drain the rice and transfer it to a steamer lined with cheesecloth or a clean kitchen towel. Steam the rice over medium-high heat for about 20-25 minutes, or until it's cooked through and tender.
3. While the rice is steaming, prepare the coconut sauce. In a saucepan, combine the coconut milk, granulated sugar, and salt. Heat the mixture over medium heat, stirring occasionally, until the sugar has dissolved and the mixture is smooth. Remove from heat and set aside.
4. Once the rice is cooked, transfer it to a mixing bowl. Pour about 3/4 of the coconut sauce over the rice, reserving the rest for serving.
5. Use a spatula or wooden spoon to gently fold the coconut sauce into the rice until it's well coated and sticky. Let the rice sit for 10-15 minutes to absorb the coconut sauce.
6. To serve, place a mound of sticky rice on a plate or in a bowl. Arrange sliced mangoes alongside or on top of the rice.
7. Drizzle some of the reserved coconut sauce over the mango sticky rice. Optionally, garnish with toasted sesame seeds or mung beans for added texture and flavor.
8. Serve the mango sticky rice warm or at room temperature. Optionally, you can drizzle extra coconut milk over the top for extra richness.

Enjoy your delicious mango sticky rice, a perfect combination of sweet, creamy, and fragrant flavors! It's a delightful dessert that's sure to impress.

Raspberry Lemon Bars

Ingredients:

For the Shortbread Crust:

- 1 cup all-purpose flour
- 1/2 cup unsalted butter, softened
- 1/4 cup granulated sugar
- Pinch of salt

For the Raspberry Lemon Filling:

- 1 cup fresh raspberries
- 1/2 cup granulated sugar
- 2 large eggs
- 1/4 cup freshly squeezed lemon juice
- 2 tablespoons lemon zest
- 2 tablespoons all-purpose flour
- Powdered sugar, for dusting (optional)

Instructions:

For the Shortbread Crust:

1. Preheat your oven to 350°F (175°C). Grease an 8x8-inch baking dish or line it with parchment paper, leaving an overhang on the sides for easy removal.
2. In a mixing bowl, cream together the softened butter and granulated sugar until light and fluffy.
3. Gradually add the all-purpose flour and salt to the butter mixture, mixing until a dough forms.
4. Press the dough evenly into the bottom of the prepared baking dish.
5. Bake the crust in the preheated oven for 15-20 minutes, or until lightly golden brown. Remove from the oven and let it cool slightly while you prepare the filling.

For the Raspberry Lemon Filling:

1. In a blender or food processor, puree the fresh raspberries until smooth. Strain the raspberry puree through a fine mesh sieve to remove the seeds, if desired.
2. In a mixing bowl, whisk together the strained raspberry puree, granulated sugar, eggs, lemon juice, lemon zest, and all-purpose flour until smooth and well combined.
3. Pour the raspberry lemon filling over the partially baked shortbread crust.
4. Return the baking dish to the oven and bake for an additional 20-25 minutes, or until the filling is set and the edges are lightly golden brown.

5. Remove the raspberry lemon bars from the oven and let them cool completely in the baking dish.
6. Once cooled, refrigerate the bars for at least 1-2 hours to chill and set.
7. Once chilled, use the parchment paper overhang to lift the bars out of the baking dish. Dust with powdered sugar, if desired, and cut into squares.
8. Serve and enjoy your delicious raspberry lemon bars!

These raspberry lemon bars are bursting with fruity flavor and make for a perfect sweet treat for any occasion. They're great for dessert tables, afternoon tea, or just as a special indulgence.

Blueberry Lemon Bundt Cake

Ingredients:

For the Cake:

- 2 cups all-purpose flour
- 1 teaspoon baking powder
- 1/2 teaspoon baking soda
- 1/2 teaspoon salt
- 1 cup unsalted butter, softened
- 1 1/4 cups granulated sugar
- 3 large eggs
- 1/2 cup sour cream
- 1/4 cup freshly squeezed lemon juice
- 2 tablespoons lemon zest
- 1 teaspoon vanilla extract
- 1 1/2 cups fresh or frozen blueberries (if using frozen, do not thaw)

For the Glaze:

- 1 cup powdered sugar
- 2-3 tablespoons freshly squeezed lemon juice
- 1 teaspoon lemon zest (optional)

Instructions:

1. Preheat your oven to 350°F (175°C). Grease and flour a 10-cup bundt pan, ensuring it's well coated to prevent sticking.
2. In a medium mixing bowl, whisk together the all-purpose flour, baking powder, baking soda, and salt. Set aside.
3. In a large mixing bowl, cream together the softened butter and granulated sugar until light and fluffy.
4. Add the eggs, one at a time, beating well after each addition.
5. Stir in the sour cream, freshly squeezed lemon juice, lemon zest, and vanilla extract until well combined.
6. Gradually add the dry ingredients to the wet ingredients, mixing until just combined.
7. Gently fold in the blueberries until evenly distributed throughout the batter.
8. Pour the batter into the prepared bundt pan, spreading it out evenly.
9. Bake in the preheated oven for 45-55 minutes, or until a toothpick inserted into the center comes out clean.
10. Remove the cake from the oven and let it cool in the pan for 10 minutes before transferring it to a wire rack to cool completely.

For the Glaze:

1. In a small mixing bowl, whisk together the powdered sugar, freshly squeezed lemon juice, and lemon zest until smooth and well combined.
2. Once the cake has cooled completely, drizzle the glaze over the top of the cake.
3. Allow the glaze to set for a few minutes before slicing and serving.

Enjoy your delicious blueberry lemon bundt cake! It's perfect for serving as a dessert or for enjoying with a cup of tea or coffee. The combination of blueberries and lemon creates a refreshing and irresistible flavor that's sure to please.

Pear Gingerbread Cake

Ingredients:

For the Cake:

- 2 cups all-purpose flour
- 1 teaspoon baking soda
- 1/2 teaspoon baking powder
- 1/2 teaspoon salt
- 2 teaspoons ground ginger
- 1 teaspoon ground cinnamon
- 1/4 teaspoon ground cloves
- 1/4 teaspoon ground nutmeg
- 1/2 cup unsalted butter, melted
- 1/2 cup granulated sugar
- 1/2 cup molasses
- 2 large eggs
- 1 teaspoon vanilla extract
- 1 cup buttermilk

For the Pears:

- 2 ripe pears, peeled, cored, and sliced
- 1 tablespoon unsalted butter
- 2 tablespoons brown sugar
- 1 teaspoon ground cinnamon

Optional Garnish:

- Powdered sugar, for dusting

Instructions:

For the Cake:

1. Preheat your oven to 350°F (175°C). Grease and flour a 9x9-inch square baking pan or line it with parchment paper.
2. In a medium mixing bowl, whisk together the all-purpose flour, baking soda, baking powder, salt, ground ginger, ground cinnamon, ground cloves, and ground nutmeg.
3. In a large mixing bowl, whisk together the melted butter, granulated sugar, molasses, eggs, and vanilla extract until well combined.
4. Gradually add the dry ingredients to the wet ingredients, alternating with the buttermilk, and mixing until just combined. Be careful not to overmix.
5. Pour the batter into the prepared baking pan, spreading it out evenly.

For the Pears:

1. In a small saucepan, melt the unsalted butter over medium heat.
2. Add the sliced pears, brown sugar, and ground cinnamon to the saucepan. Cook, stirring occasionally, until the pears are softened and caramelized, about 5-7 minutes.
3. Arrange the caramelized pears on top of the cake batter in the baking pan.

Baking:

1. Bake the cake in the preheated oven for 35-40 minutes, or until a toothpick inserted into the center comes out clean.
2. Remove the cake from the oven and let it cool in the pan for 10 minutes before transferring it to a wire rack to cool completely.

Optional Garnish:

1. Once the cake has cooled completely, dust the top with powdered sugar for a decorative touch.

Enjoy your delicious pear gingerbread cake! It's perfect for serving as a festive dessert during the holiday season or anytime you're craving a cozy and comforting treat.

Blackberry Pie Bars

Ingredients:

For the Crust and Crumble Topping:

- 2 cups all-purpose flour
- 1 cup granulated sugar
- 1/4 teaspoon salt
- 1 cup unsalted butter, cold and cubed

For the Blackberry Filling:

- 4 cups fresh blackberries
- 1/2 cup granulated sugar
- 2 tablespoons cornstarch
- 1 tablespoon freshly squeezed lemon juice
- 1 teaspoon lemon zest

Instructions:

1. Preheat your oven to 350°F (175°C). Grease a 9x13-inch baking dish or line it with parchment paper, leaving an overhang on the sides for easy removal.
2. In a large mixing bowl, combine the all-purpose flour, granulated sugar, and salt for the crust and crumble topping.
3. Add the cold cubed butter to the flour mixture. Use a pastry cutter or fork to cut the butter into the dry ingredients until the mixture resembles coarse crumbs.
4. Reserve about 1 1/2 cups of the crumble mixture for the topping. Press the remaining mixture evenly into the bottom of the prepared baking dish to form the crust.
5. In another mixing bowl, combine the fresh blackberries, granulated sugar, cornstarch, lemon juice, and lemon zest for the blackberry filling. Toss until the blackberries are evenly coated.
6. Spread the blackberry filling evenly over the crust in the baking dish.
7. Sprinkle the reserved crumble mixture evenly over the top of the blackberry filling to form the crumble topping.
8. Bake in the preheated oven for 45-55 minutes, or until the crust and crumble topping are golden brown and the blackberry filling is bubbling.
9. Remove the blackberry pie bars from the oven and let them cool completely in the baking dish.
10. Once cooled, use the parchment paper overhang to lift the bars out of the baking dish. Cut into squares or bars.
11. Serve and enjoy your delicious blackberry pie bars!

These blackberry pie bars are perfect for serving as a dessert or sweet treat for any occasion. They're great for picnics, potlucks, or enjoying with a scoop of vanilla ice cream for an extra indulgent treat.

Peach Melba

Ingredients:

- 4 ripe peaches, peeled and halved
- 1/2 cup granulated sugar
- 1 cup water
- 1 cup fresh raspberries
- 2 tablespoons powdered sugar
- 1 tablespoon lemon juice
- Vanilla ice cream, for serving
- Fresh mint leaves, for garnish (optional)

Instructions:

For the Poached Peaches:

1. In a saucepan, combine the granulated sugar and water. Bring to a simmer over medium heat, stirring until the sugar is dissolved.
2. Add the peeled and halved peaches to the simmering syrup. Reduce the heat to low and poach the peaches for about 10-15 minutes, or until they are tender but still hold their shape.
3. Remove the poached peaches from the syrup using a slotted spoon and transfer them to a plate. Let them cool slightly.

For the Raspberry Sauce:

1. In a blender or food processor, puree the fresh raspberries until smooth.
2. Strain the raspberry puree through a fine mesh sieve into a bowl to remove the seeds.
3. Stir in the powdered sugar and lemon juice until well combined. Adjust the sweetness and tartness to taste, adding more powdered sugar if desired.

Assembly:

1. Place a poached peach half in the center of each serving plate or bowl.
2. Drizzle the raspberry sauce over the poached peaches.
3. Serve each peach with a scoop of vanilla ice cream on the side.
4. Garnish with fresh mint leaves, if desired, for a pop of color and flavor.

Enjoy your delicious Peach Melba! It's a timeless dessert that's perfect for showcasing the flavors of ripe summer peaches and tangy raspberries, balanced by creamy vanilla ice cream.

Apricot Galette

Ingredients:

For the Pastry:

- 1 1/4 cups all-purpose flour
- 1/2 teaspoon granulated sugar
- 1/4 teaspoon salt
- 1/2 cup unsalted butter, cold and cut into cubes
- 3-4 tablespoons ice water

For the Filling:

- 1 pound fresh apricots, pitted and sliced
- 2 tablespoons granulated sugar
- 1 tablespoon cornstarch
- 1 tablespoon freshly squeezed lemon juice
- 1 teaspoon lemon zest
- 1/4 teaspoon ground cinnamon (optional)
- 1 tablespoon apricot jam (for glazing)
- 1 tablespoon water (for glazing)
- Powdered sugar, for dusting (optional)

Instructions:

For the Pastry:

1. In a large mixing bowl, combine the all-purpose flour, granulated sugar, and salt.
2. Add the cold cubed butter to the flour mixture. Use a pastry cutter or fork to cut the butter into the dry ingredients until the mixture resembles coarse crumbs.
3. Gradually add the ice water, one tablespoon at a time, mixing until the dough comes together and forms a ball. Be careful not to overwork the dough.
4. Flatten the dough into a disk, wrap it in plastic wrap, and refrigerate for at least 30 minutes to chill.

For the Filling:

1. In a mixing bowl, combine the sliced apricots, granulated sugar, cornstarch, lemon juice, lemon zest, and ground cinnamon (if using). Toss until the apricots are evenly coated.

Assembly:

1. Preheat your oven to 375°F (190°C). Line a baking sheet with parchment paper.
2. On a lightly floured surface, roll out the chilled dough into a circle about 12 inches in diameter and 1/8 inch thick.

3. Transfer the rolled-out dough to the prepared baking sheet.
4. Arrange the sliced apricots in the center of the dough, leaving about a 2-inch border around the edges.
5. Gently fold the edges of the dough over the apricots, overlapping slightly and pleating as you go.
6. In a small saucepan, heat the apricot jam and water over low heat until melted and smooth.
7. Brush the melted apricot jam mixture over the apricots and the edges of the dough.
8. Bake the galette in the preheated oven for 30-35 minutes, or until the crust is golden brown and the filling is bubbling.
9. Remove the galette from the oven and let it cool slightly on the baking sheet.
10. Once cooled, transfer the galette to a serving platter. Dust with powdered sugar, if desired, before serving.

Enjoy your delicious apricot galette! Serve it warm or at room temperature, optionally with a scoop of vanilla ice cream or a dollop of whipped cream.

Grapefruit Sorbet

Ingredients:

- 3 cups fresh grapefruit juice (from about 4-5 large grapefruits)
- 3/4 cup granulated sugar
- 1/2 cup water
- 1 tablespoon freshly squeezed lemon juice (optional, for added tartness)

Instructions:

1. Begin by preparing the grapefruit juice. Cut the grapefruits in half and juice them using a citrus juicer or a manual juicing method until you have 3 cups of fresh grapefruit juice. Strain the juice through a fine mesh sieve to remove any pulp or seeds.
2. In a small saucepan, combine the granulated sugar and water. Heat the mixture over medium heat, stirring constantly, until the sugar is completely dissolved. This will create a simple syrup.
3. Once the sugar is dissolved, remove the syrup from the heat and let it cool to room temperature.
4. In a large mixing bowl, combine the fresh grapefruit juice with the cooled simple syrup. Add the freshly squeezed lemon juice if desired for added tartness. Stir until well combined.
5. Pour the grapefruit mixture into an ice cream maker and churn according to the manufacturer's instructions until it reaches a soft sorbet consistency. This typically takes about 20-25 minutes.
6. Transfer the churned sorbet into a freezer-safe container and freeze for an additional 2-4 hours, or until firm.
7. Once the sorbet is firm, scoop it into serving dishes and enjoy!

This grapefruit sorbet is refreshingly tart and perfect for cooling down on a hot day. You can also garnish it with fresh mint leaves or a slice of grapefruit for an extra touch of elegance.

Lemon Poppy Seed Cake

Ingredients:

For the Cake:

- 1 1/2 cups all-purpose flour
- 1/2 cup granulated sugar
- 2 tablespoons poppy seeds
- 2 teaspoons baking powder
- 1/4 teaspoon salt
- 1/2 cup unsalted butter, softened
- 2 large eggs
- 1/2 cup milk
- 2 tablespoons freshly squeezed lemon juice
- Zest of 1 lemon
- 1 teaspoon vanilla extract

For the Lemon Glaze:

- 1 cup powdered sugar
- 2-3 tablespoons freshly squeezed lemon juice
- Zest of 1 lemon (optional, for extra lemon flavor)

Instructions:

For the Cake:

1. Preheat your oven to 350°F (175°C). Grease and flour a 9x5-inch loaf pan or line it with parchment paper.
2. In a mixing bowl, whisk together the all-purpose flour, granulated sugar, poppy seeds, baking powder, and salt until well combined.
3. In another mixing bowl, cream together the softened butter and granulated sugar until light and fluffy.
4. Add the eggs, one at a time, beating well after each addition.
5. Stir in the milk, freshly squeezed lemon juice, lemon zest, and vanilla extract until well combined.
6. Gradually add the dry ingredients to the wet ingredients, mixing until just combined. Be careful not to overmix.
7. Pour the batter into the prepared loaf pan, spreading it out evenly.
8. Bake in the preheated oven for 45-50 minutes, or until a toothpick inserted into the center comes out clean.
9. Remove the cake from the oven and let it cool in the pan for 10 minutes before transferring it to a wire rack to cool completely.

For the Lemon Glaze:

1. In a small mixing bowl, whisk together the powdered sugar and freshly squeezed lemon juice until smooth.
2. If desired, stir in the lemon zest for extra lemon flavor.
3. Once the cake has cooled completely, drizzle the lemon glaze over the top.
4. Let the glaze set for a few minutes before slicing and serving.

Enjoy your delicious lemon poppy seed cake! It's perfect for serving as a dessert or for enjoying with a cup of tea or coffee. The combination of tart lemon and crunchy poppy seeds creates a delightful flavor and texture.

Cherry Chocolate Chip Cookies

Ingredients:

- 1/2 cup unsalted butter, softened
- 1/2 cup granulated sugar
- 1/2 cup brown sugar, packed
- 1 large egg
- 1 teaspoon vanilla extract
- 1 1/2 cups all-purpose flour
- 1/2 teaspoon baking soda
- 1/2 teaspoon salt
- 3/4 cup semi-sweet chocolate chips
- 3/4 cup dried cherries, chopped

Instructions:

1. Preheat your oven to 350°F (175°C). Line a baking sheet with parchment paper.
2. In a large mixing bowl, cream together the softened butter, granulated sugar, and brown sugar until light and fluffy.
3. Add the egg and vanilla extract to the creamed mixture and beat until well combined.
4. In a separate bowl, whisk together the all-purpose flour, baking soda, and salt.
5. Gradually add the dry ingredients to the wet ingredients, mixing until just combined.
6. Fold in the semi-sweet chocolate chips and chopped dried cherries until evenly distributed throughout the dough.
7. Using a spoon or cookie scoop, drop rounded tablespoons of dough onto the prepared baking sheet, spacing them about 2 inches apart.
8. Bake in the preheated oven for 10-12 minutes, or until the edges are golden brown and the centers are set.
9. Remove the cookies from the oven and let them cool on the baking sheet for a few minutes before transferring them to a wire rack to cool completely.

Enjoy your delicious cherry chocolate chip cookies! They're perfect for enjoying as a sweet treat with a glass of milk or sharing with friends and family.

Watermelon Sorbet

Ingredients:

- 4 cups of seedless watermelon, cubed
- 1/2 cup granulated sugar
- 1 tablespoon freshly squeezed lime juice (optional, for added brightness)

Instructions:

1. Place the cubed watermelon in a blender or food processor and blend until smooth.
2. Pour the watermelon puree through a fine mesh sieve into a large mixing bowl to remove any pulp and seeds.
3. In a small saucepan, combine the granulated sugar with 1/2 cup of water. Heat the mixture over medium heat, stirring constantly, until the sugar is completely dissolved. This will create a simple syrup.
4. Once the sugar is dissolved, remove the simple syrup from the heat and let it cool to room temperature.
5. Once cooled, add the simple syrup to the watermelon puree in the mixing bowl. Stir until well combined.
6. Optionally, add the freshly squeezed lime juice to the mixture for added brightness and a hint of tartness. Stir to combine.
7. Pour the watermelon mixture into an ice cream maker and churn according to the manufacturer's instructions until it reaches a soft sorbet consistency. This typically takes about 20-25 minutes.
8. Transfer the churned sorbet into a freezer-safe container and freeze for an additional 2-4 hours, or until firm.
9. Once the sorbet is firm, scoop it into serving dishes and enjoy!

This watermelon sorbet is perfect for cooling down on a hot day. It's light, refreshing, and bursting with sweet watermelon flavor. You can also garnish it with fresh mint leaves or a slice of lime for an extra touch of freshness.

Kiwi Pavlova

Ingredients:

For the Meringue:

- 4 large egg whites, at room temperature
- 1 cup granulated sugar
- 1 teaspoon cornstarch
- 1 teaspoon white vinegar
- 1/2 teaspoon vanilla extract

For the Topping:

- 1 cup heavy cream, chilled
- 2 tablespoons powdered sugar
- 4-5 ripe kiwi fruits, peeled and sliced
- Fresh mint leaves, for garnish (optional)

Instructions:

For the Meringue:

1. Preheat your oven to 250°F (120°C). Line a baking sheet with parchment paper.
2. In a clean, dry mixing bowl, beat the egg whites with an electric mixer on medium speed until soft peaks form.
3. Gradually add the granulated sugar, one tablespoon at a time, while continuing to beat the egg whites on high speed. Beat until stiff, glossy peaks form.
4. Gently fold in the cornstarch, white vinegar, and vanilla extract until just combined.
5. Spoon the meringue mixture onto the prepared baking sheet, forming a circle or oval shape, depending on your preference. Use the back of a spoon to create a shallow well in the center of the meringue for the toppings.
6. Bake the meringue in the preheated oven for 1 hour and 15 minutes to 1 hour and 30 minutes, or until the meringue is crisp on the outside and slightly chewy on the inside. Turn off the oven and let the meringue cool completely inside the oven with the door slightly ajar.

For the Topping:

1. In a mixing bowl, whip the chilled heavy cream and powdered sugar together until stiff peaks form.
2. Spoon the whipped cream onto the cooled meringue, spreading it out evenly.
3. Arrange the sliced kiwi fruits on top of the whipped cream.
4. Garnish with fresh mint leaves, if desired, for an extra touch of freshness.

Enjoy your delicious kiwi pavlova! It's a perfect dessert for showcasing the natural sweetness of ripe kiwi fruits and the airy texture of the meringue. Serve it chilled and enjoy the delightful combination of flavors and textures.

Banana Pudding

Ingredients:

- 3/4 cup granulated sugar
- 1/4 cup cornstarch
- 1/4 teaspoon salt
- 3 cups whole milk
- 4 large egg yolks
- 2 tablespoons unsalted butter
- 1 teaspoon vanilla extract
- 3 ripe bananas, sliced
- 1 (11-ounce) box of vanilla wafers
- Whipped cream, for serving (optional)

Instructions:

1. In a medium saucepan, whisk together the granulated sugar, cornstarch, and salt.
2. Gradually whisk in the whole milk until smooth.
3. Cook the mixture over medium heat, stirring constantly, until it thickens and comes to a boil. This will take about 5-7 minutes.
4. Once the mixture has thickened, reduce the heat to low.
5. In a separate bowl, lightly beat the egg yolks. Gradually whisk in about 1/2 cup of the hot milk mixture to temper the eggs.
6. Pour the tempered egg mixture back into the saucepan with the remaining hot milk mixture, whisking constantly.
7. Cook the pudding over low heat, stirring constantly, for an additional 2-3 minutes, until thickened.
8. Remove the saucepan from the heat and stir in the unsalted butter and vanilla extract until the butter is melted and the mixture is smooth.
9. Let the pudding cool for a few minutes.
10. In a large serving dish or individual serving cups, layer the vanilla wafers, sliced bananas, and pudding mixture.
11. Continue layering until all ingredients are used, ending with a layer of pudding on top.
12. Cover the pudding with plastic wrap, pressing it directly onto the surface to prevent a skin from forming.
13. Refrigerate the banana pudding for at least 4 hours, or overnight, to allow the flavors to meld and the pudding to set.
14. Before serving, garnish the banana pudding with additional sliced bananas and whipped cream, if desired.

Enjoy your delicious homemade banana pudding! It's a comforting and nostalgic dessert that's perfect for any occasion.

Coconut Lime Bars

Ingredients:

For the Shortbread Crust:

- 1 1/2 cups all-purpose flour
- 1/2 cup granulated sugar
- 1/4 teaspoon salt
- 3/4 cup unsalted butter, cold and cubed

For the Coconut Lime Filling:

- 4 large eggs
- 1 1/2 cups granulated sugar
- 1/2 cup freshly squeezed lime juice
- Zest of 2 limes
- 1/4 cup all-purpose flour
- 1/2 cup shredded coconut
- Powdered sugar, for dusting (optional)

Instructions:

For the Shortbread Crust:

1. Preheat your oven to 350°F (175°C). Grease a 9x13-inch baking dish or line it with parchment paper.
2. In a large mixing bowl, whisk together the all-purpose flour, granulated sugar, and salt.
3. Cut in the cold cubed butter using a pastry cutter or fork until the mixture resembles coarse crumbs.
4. Press the mixture evenly into the bottom of the prepared baking dish.
5. Bake the crust in the preheated oven for 15-18 minutes, or until lightly golden brown around the edges. Remove from the oven and set aside.

For the Coconut Lime Filling:

1. In a mixing bowl, beat the eggs until well combined.
2. Gradually add the granulated sugar, lime juice, and lime zest, mixing until smooth.
3. Stir in the all-purpose flour and shredded coconut until well combined.
4. Pour the filling over the pre-baked shortbread crust, spreading it out evenly.
5. Return the baking dish to the oven and bake for an additional 20-25 minutes, or until the filling is set and the edges are lightly golden brown.
6. Remove the baking dish from the oven and let the bars cool completely in the dish.
7. Once cooled, refrigerate the bars for at least 1-2 hours to chill and set.
8. Before serving, dust the coconut lime bars with powdered sugar, if desired.

9. Cut into squares and serve chilled.

Enjoy your delicious coconut lime bars! They're perfect for serving as a refreshing dessert or sweet snack, especially during the warmer months. The tangy lime and sweet coconut flavors are sure to be a hit with family and friends.

Orange Creamsicle Pie

Ingredients:

For the Crust:

- 1 1/2 cups graham cracker crumbs
- 1/4 cup granulated sugar
- 6 tablespoons unsalted butter, melted

For the Filling:

- 1 (14-ounce) can sweetened condensed milk
- 3/4 cup freshly squeezed orange juice
- Zest of 1 orange
- 1 teaspoon vanilla extract
- 2 cups whipped cream or whipped topping

For Garnish (optional):

- Additional whipped cream or whipped topping
- Orange slices or zest

Instructions:

For the Crust:

1. Preheat your oven to 350°F (175°C).
2. In a mixing bowl, combine the graham cracker crumbs, granulated sugar, and melted butter. Stir until the mixture resembles coarse sand and holds together when pressed.
3. Press the crumb mixture evenly into the bottom and up the sides of a 9-inch pie dish.
4. Bake the crust in the preheated oven for 8-10 minutes, or until lightly golden brown. Remove from the oven and let it cool completely.

For the Filling:

1. In a large mixing bowl, whisk together the sweetened condensed milk, freshly squeezed orange juice, orange zest, and vanilla extract until smooth and well combined.
2. Gently fold in the whipped cream or whipped topping until fully incorporated.
3. Pour the filling into the cooled graham cracker crust, spreading it out evenly.
4. Refrigerate the pie for at least 4 hours, or until set.

For Garnish (optional):

1. Before serving, garnish the chilled pie with additional whipped cream or whipped topping.

2. Optionally, garnish with orange slices or zest for a pop of color and extra orange flavor.

Enjoy your delicious orange creamsicle pie! It's a refreshing and creamy dessert that's perfect for any occasion, especially during the warmer months. The combination of tangy orange and creamy vanilla is sure to be a hit with family and friends.

Mango Coconut Rice Pudding

Ingredients:

- 1 cup jasmine rice (or any other medium-grain rice)
- 1 (14-ounce) can coconut milk
- 2 cups whole milk
- 1/2 cup granulated sugar
- 1 teaspoon vanilla extract
- 2 ripe mangoes, peeled and diced
- Shredded coconut, toasted (for garnish, optional)
- Fresh mint leaves (for garnish, optional)

Instructions:

1. Rinse the jasmine rice under cold water until the water runs clear. This helps remove excess starch and prevents the rice from becoming too sticky.
2. In a medium saucepan, combine the rinsed rice, coconut milk, whole milk, and granulated sugar.
3. Bring the mixture to a gentle boil over medium heat, stirring occasionally to prevent the rice from sticking to the bottom of the pan.
4. Once the mixture reaches a boil, reduce the heat to low and let it simmer, uncovered, for about 20-25 minutes, or until the rice is tender and the mixture has thickened to a creamy consistency. Stir occasionally to ensure even cooking.
5. Remove the saucepan from the heat and stir in the vanilla extract.
6. Let the rice pudding cool slightly, then transfer it to a serving dish or individual serving bowls.
7. Cover the rice pudding with plastic wrap, pressing it directly onto the surface to prevent a skin from forming, and refrigerate for at least 1 hour, or until chilled.
8. Once the rice pudding has chilled, spoon the diced mangoes over the top.
9. Optionally, garnish with toasted shredded coconut and fresh mint leaves for extra flavor and presentation.
10. Serve chilled and enjoy your delicious mango coconut rice pudding!

This creamy and tropical dessert is perfect for serving at summer gatherings or anytime you're craving a taste of the tropics. The combination of coconut milk, sweet mangoes, and creamy rice pudding is sure to be a hit with family and friends.

Raspberry Swirl Cheesecake

Ingredients:

For the Crust:

- 1 1/2 cups graham cracker crumbs
- 1/4 cup granulated sugar
- 1/3 cup unsalted butter, melted

For the Cheesecake Filling:

- 24 ounces cream cheese, softened
- 1 cup granulated sugar
- 3 large eggs
- 1 teaspoon vanilla extract
- 1/4 cup sour cream
- 1/4 cup heavy cream

For the Raspberry Swirl:

- 1 cup fresh or frozen raspberries
- 2 tablespoons granulated sugar
- 1 tablespoon lemon juice

Instructions:

For the Crust:

1. Preheat your oven to 325°F (160°C). Grease a 9-inch springform pan and line the bottom with parchment paper.
2. In a mixing bowl, combine the graham cracker crumbs, granulated sugar, and melted butter. Stir until the mixture resembles coarse sand and holds together when pressed.
3. Press the crumb mixture evenly into the bottom of the prepared springform pan.
4. Bake the crust in the preheated oven for 10 minutes. Remove from the oven and let it cool while you prepare the cheesecake filling.

For the Cheesecake Filling:

1. In a large mixing bowl, beat the softened cream cheese and granulated sugar together until smooth and creamy.
2. Add the eggs one at a time, beating well after each addition.
3. Stir in the vanilla extract, sour cream, and heavy cream until well combined and smooth.

For the Raspberry Swirl:

1. In a small saucepan, combine the raspberries, granulated sugar, and lemon juice.
2. Cook the mixture over medium heat, stirring occasionally, until the raspberries break down and the mixture thickens slightly, about 5-7 minutes.
3. Remove the saucepan from the heat and let the raspberry mixture cool slightly.
4. Once cooled, strain the raspberry mixture through a fine mesh sieve to remove the seeds. You should be left with a smooth raspberry puree.

Assembly:

1. Pour the cheesecake filling over the cooled crust in the springform pan.
2. Spoon dollops of the raspberry puree over the top of the cheesecake filling.
3. Use a knife or toothpick to swirl the raspberry puree into the cheesecake filling, creating a marbled effect.
4. Place the springform pan on a baking sheet and bake the cheesecake in the preheated oven for 45-50 minutes, or until the edges are set and the center is slightly jiggly.
5. Turn off the oven and let the cheesecake cool in the oven with the door slightly ajar for 1 hour.
6. Remove the cheesecake from the oven and let it cool completely at room temperature.
7. Once cooled, refrigerate the cheesecake for at least 4 hours, or overnight, to chill and set.
8. Before serving, run a knife around the edge of the springform pan to loosen the cheesecake. Remove the sides of the pan.
9. Slice the cheesecake into wedges and serve chilled.

Enjoy your delicious raspberry swirl cheesecake! It's a perfect dessert for any occasion, with its creamy texture and tangy raspberry swirls delighting your taste buds with every bite.

Strawberry Balsamic Ice Cream

Ingredients:

- 2 cups fresh strawberries, hulled and chopped
- 1/4 cup balsamic vinegar
- 1/2 cup granulated sugar
- 2 cups heavy cream
- 1 cup whole milk
- 4 large egg yolks
- 2/3 cup granulated sugar
- 1 teaspoon vanilla extract

Instructions:

For the Strawberry Balsamic Compote:

1. In a small saucepan, combine the chopped strawberries, balsamic vinegar, and 1/2 cup granulated sugar.
2. Cook the mixture over medium heat, stirring occasionally, until the strawberries break down and the mixture thickens slightly, about 10-15 minutes.
3. Remove the saucepan from the heat and let the strawberry balsamic compote cool completely. You can transfer it to a bowl and refrigerate it to speed up the cooling process.

For the Ice Cream Base:

1. In a medium saucepan, combine the heavy cream, whole milk, and 2/3 cup granulated sugar.
2. Heat the mixture over medium heat, stirring occasionally, until it reaches a simmer. Remove from heat.
3. In a separate mixing bowl, whisk the egg yolks until smooth.
4. Gradually pour the hot cream mixture into the egg yolks, whisking constantly, to temper the eggs.
5. Once tempered, pour the mixture back into the saucepan.
6. Cook the mixture over medium heat, stirring constantly, until it thickens and coats the back of a spoon, about 5-7 minutes. Do not let it boil.
7. Remove the saucepan from the heat and stir in the vanilla extract.
8. Strain the ice cream base through a fine mesh sieve into a clean bowl to remove any lumps.
9. Let the ice cream base cool to room temperature, then cover it with plastic wrap, pressing it directly onto the surface to prevent a skin from forming. Refrigerate the mixture until completely chilled, preferably overnight.

Assembling the Ice Cream:

1. Once the ice cream base and strawberry balsamic compote are completely chilled, churn the ice cream base in an ice cream maker according to the manufacturer's instructions.
2. When the ice cream is almost done churning, add spoonfuls of the strawberry balsamic compote into the ice cream maker and continue churning until the compote is evenly distributed throughout the ice cream.
3. Transfer the churned ice cream to a freezer-safe container and freeze for at least 4 hours, or until firm.
4. Before serving, let the ice cream sit at room temperature for a few minutes to soften slightly.
5. Scoop the strawberry balsamic ice cream into bowls or cones and enjoy!

This strawberry balsamic ice cream is a unique and delicious treat that's perfect for enjoying during the warmer months or anytime you're craving a refreshing dessert with a twist!

Pineapple Coconut Crisp

Ingredients:

For the Filling:

- 4 cups fresh pineapple, peeled, cored, and diced (or 1 can of pineapple chunks, drained)
- 1/4 cup granulated sugar
- 2 tablespoons all-purpose flour
- 1 teaspoon vanilla extract
- Zest of 1 lemon (optional)

For the Crisp Topping:

- 1 cup old-fashioned rolled oats
- 1/2 cup all-purpose flour
- 1/2 cup shredded coconut
- 1/2 cup packed brown sugar
- 1/2 teaspoon ground cinnamon
- 1/4 teaspoon salt
- 1/2 cup unsalted butter, melted

Instructions:

1. Preheat your oven to 350°F (175°C). Grease a 9x9-inch baking dish or similar-sized oven-safe dish.
2. In a large mixing bowl, combine the diced pineapple, granulated sugar, all-purpose flour, vanilla extract, and lemon zest (if using). Stir until the pineapple is evenly coated with the sugar mixture.
3. Transfer the pineapple mixture to the prepared baking dish and spread it out evenly.

For the Crisp Topping:

1. In a separate mixing bowl, combine the rolled oats, all-purpose flour, shredded coconut, brown sugar, ground cinnamon, and salt.
2. Pour the melted butter over the dry ingredients and mix until everything is well combined and the mixture resembles coarse crumbs.
3. Sprinkle the crisp topping evenly over the pineapple mixture in the baking dish.
4. Bake the pineapple coconut crisp in the preheated oven for 30-35 minutes, or until the topping is golden brown and the filling is bubbly.
5. Remove the crisp from the oven and let it cool for a few minutes before serving.
6. Serve warm, optionally topped with a scoop of vanilla ice cream or a dollop of whipped cream.

Enjoy your delicious pineapple coconut crisp! It's a perfect dessert for summer gatherings or any time you want to bring a taste of the tropics to your table. The combination of sweet pineapple and coconut with the crunchy topping is sure to be a hit with family and friends.

Blackberry Lime Cupcakes

Ingredients:

For the Cupcakes:

- 1 1/2 cups all-purpose flour
- 1 1/2 teaspoons baking powder
- 1/4 teaspoon salt
- 1/2 cup unsalted butter, softened
- 3/4 cup granulated sugar
- 2 large eggs
- 1 teaspoon vanilla extract
- Zest of 1 lime
- 1/4 cup freshly squeezed lime juice
- 1/2 cup whole milk

For the Blackberry Frosting:

- 1 cup fresh blackberries
- 1/4 cup unsalted butter, softened
- 2 cups powdered sugar
- 1-2 tablespoons milk or cream
- Additional blackberries, for garnish (optional)

Instructions:

For the Cupcakes:

1. Preheat your oven to 350°F (175°C). Line a muffin tin with cupcake liners.
2. In a medium mixing bowl, whisk together the all-purpose flour, baking powder, and salt.
3. In a large mixing bowl, cream together the softened butter and granulated sugar until light and fluffy.
4. Add the eggs one at a time, beating well after each addition. Then, mix in the vanilla extract and lime zest.
5. Gradually add the dry ingredients to the wet ingredients, alternating with the freshly squeezed lime juice and whole milk, beginning and ending with the dry ingredients. Mix until just combined.
6. Divide the cupcake batter evenly among the prepared muffin cups, filling each cup about 2/3 full.
7. Bake the cupcakes in the preheated oven for 18-20 minutes, or until a toothpick inserted into the center comes out clean.
8. Remove the cupcakes from the oven and let them cool in the muffin tin for a few minutes before transferring them to a wire rack to cool completely.

For the Blackberry Frosting:

1. In a blender or food processor, puree the fresh blackberries until smooth. Strain the puree through a fine mesh sieve to remove the seeds, if desired.

2. In a large mixing bowl, beat the softened butter until smooth and creamy.
3. Gradually add the powdered sugar to the butter, beating until well combined.
4. Mix in the blackberry puree, starting with 1/4 cup and adding more as needed to achieve the desired consistency.
5. If the frosting is too thick, add milk or cream, one tablespoon at a time, until it reaches the desired consistency.

Assembly:

1. Once the cupcakes are completely cooled, frost them with the blackberry frosting using a piping bag or offset spatula.
2. Garnish each cupcake with a fresh blackberry, if desired.
3. Serve and enjoy your delicious blackberry lime cupcakes!

These cupcakes are perfect for any occasion, with their bright and refreshing flavor. They're sure to be a hit with anyone who loves the combination of tangy lime and sweet blackberries.

Peach Melba Crumble

Ingredients:

For the Filling:

- 4 cups sliced fresh peaches (about 4-5 peaches)
- 1 cup fresh raspberries
- 1/4 cup granulated sugar
- 2 tablespoons cornstarch
- 1 tablespoon lemon juice

For the Crumble Topping:

- 1 cup old-fashioned rolled oats
- 1/2 cup all-purpose flour
- 1/2 cup packed brown sugar
- 1/2 teaspoon ground cinnamon
- 1/4 teaspoon salt
- 1/2 cup unsalted butter, cold and cubed

Instructions:

1. Preheat your oven to 350°F (175°C). Grease a 9x9-inch baking dish or similar-sized oven-safe dish.
2. In a large mixing bowl, combine the sliced peaches, raspberries, granulated sugar, cornstarch, and lemon juice. Stir until the fruit is evenly coated with the sugar mixture.
3. Transfer the fruit mixture to the prepared baking dish and spread it out evenly.

For the Crumble Topping:

1. In a separate mixing bowl, combine the rolled oats, all-purpose flour, packed brown sugar, ground cinnamon, and salt.
2. Add the cold cubed butter to the dry ingredients.
3. Using your fingers or a pastry cutter, work the butter into the dry ingredients until the mixture resembles coarse crumbs and the butter is evenly distributed.

Assembly:

1. Sprinkle the crumble topping evenly over the fruit mixture in the baking dish.
2. Place the baking dish on a baking sheet to catch any drips.
3. Bake the peach melba crumble in the preheated oven for 40-45 minutes, or until the fruit is bubbly and the topping is golden brown and crisp.
4. Remove the crumble from the oven and let it cool for a few minutes before serving.
5. Serve warm, optionally topped with a scoop of vanilla ice cream or a dollop of whipped cream.

Enjoy your delicious peach melba crumble! It's a perfect dessert for summer gatherings or any time you want to enjoy the flavors of ripe peaches and tart raspberries in a comforting and satisfying treat.

Blueberry Lemon Scones

Ingredients:

- 2 cups all-purpose flour
- 1/4 cup granulated sugar

- 1 tablespoon baking powder
- 1/2 teaspoon salt
- Zest of 1 lemon
- 1/2 cup unsalted butter, cold and cubed
- 1 cup fresh or frozen blueberries
- 2/3 cup heavy cream, plus more for brushing
- 1 large egg
- 1 teaspoon vanilla extract
- Optional: coarse sugar for sprinkling on top

Instructions:

1. Preheat your oven to 400°F (200°C). Line a baking sheet with parchment paper.
2. In a large mixing bowl, whisk together the flour, granulated sugar, baking powder, salt, and lemon zest.
3. Add the cold cubed butter to the dry ingredients. Using a pastry cutter or your fingers, work the butter into the flour mixture until it resembles coarse crumbs.
4. Gently fold in the blueberries, being careful not to crush them.
5. In a separate bowl, whisk together the heavy cream, egg, and vanilla extract.
6. Pour the wet ingredients into the dry ingredients and mix until just combined. Be careful not to overmix.
7. Turn the dough out onto a lightly floured surface and gently knead it a few times until it comes together. Shape the dough into a circle about 1-inch thick.
8. Using a sharp knife or bench scraper, cut the circle into 8 wedges.
9. Place the scones on the prepared baking sheet, leaving space between them.
10. Brush the tops of the scones with a little heavy cream and sprinkle with coarse sugar, if desired.
11. Bake in the preheated oven for 15-18 minutes, or until the scones are golden brown and cooked through.
12. Remove the scones from the oven and let them cool on the baking sheet for a few minutes before transferring them to a wire rack to cool completely.

Enjoy your delicious blueberry lemon scones! Serve them warm or at room temperature with a cup of tea or coffee for a delightful breakfast or snack.

Mango Raspberry Popsicles

Ingredients:

- 1 ripe mango, peeled and diced
- 1 cup fresh or frozen raspberries

- 1/4 cup honey or maple syrup (adjust to taste)
- 1/2 cup water

Instructions:

1. In a blender or food processor, combine the diced mango, raspberries, honey or maple syrup, and water.
2. Blend until smooth and well combined. If the mixture is too thick, you can add a little more water to reach your desired consistency.
3. Taste the mixture and adjust the sweetness if necessary by adding more honey or maple syrup.
4. Once the mixture is smooth and sweetened to your liking, pour it into popsicle molds, leaving a little space at the top for expansion.
5. Insert popsicle sticks into the molds and freeze for at least 4-6 hours, or until the popsicles are completely frozen.
6. Once frozen, remove the popsicles from the molds by running them under warm water for a few seconds to loosen.
7. Serve immediately and enjoy your delicious mango raspberry popsicles!

These popsicles are not only delicious but also healthy, made with real fruit and natural sweeteners. They're perfect for cooling down on a hot day and can be enjoyed by both kids and adults alike. Feel free to experiment with different fruit combinations or add a splash of coconut milk for extra creaminess.

Raspberry Chocolate Tart

Ingredients:

For the Tart Crust:

- 1 1/4 cups all-purpose flour
- 1/4 cup cocoa powder
- 1/2 cup unsalted butter, cold and cubed
- 1/4 cup granulated sugar
- 1 large egg yolk
- 1-2 tablespoons ice water

For the Chocolate Filling:

- 8 ounces dark chocolate, chopped
- 1 cup heavy cream
- 1 tablespoon unsalted butter

For the Raspberry Topping:

- 2 cups fresh raspberries
- 2 tablespoons raspberry jam or jelly
- 1 tablespoon water

Instructions:

For the Tart Crust:

1. In a food processor, combine the flour, cocoa powder, cold cubed butter, and granulated sugar. Pulse until the mixture resembles coarse crumbs.
2. Add the egg yolk and 1 tablespoon of ice water. Pulse until the dough comes together. If the dough seems too dry, add more ice water, 1 tablespoon at a time, until it forms a cohesive ball.
3. Flatten the dough into a disk, wrap it in plastic wrap, and refrigerate for at least 30 minutes.
4. Preheat your oven to 375°F (190°C). Roll out the chilled dough on a lightly floured surface into a circle slightly larger than your tart pan.
5. Press the dough into a 9-inch tart pan with a removable bottom, trimming any excess dough from the edges.
6. Prick the bottom of the crust with a fork, then line it with parchment paper and fill it with pie weights or dried beans.
7. Blind bake the crust in the preheated oven for 15 minutes. Remove the parchment paper and pie weights, then bake for an additional 5-7 minutes, or until the crust is set and dry. Remove from the oven and let it cool completely.

For the Chocolate Filling:

1. Place the chopped dark chocolate in a heatproof bowl.
2. In a small saucepan, heat the heavy cream and butter over medium heat until it just begins to simmer.

3. Pour the hot cream mixture over the chopped chocolate and let it sit for 1-2 minutes.
4. Stir the chocolate and cream together until smooth and well combined.

Assembly:

1. Pour the chocolate filling into the cooled tart crust and spread it out evenly with a spatula.
2. Refrigerate the tart for at least 1 hour, or until the chocolate filling is set.
3. In a small saucepan, heat the raspberry jam or jelly with 1 tablespoon of water over low heat until melted and smooth.
4. Arrange the fresh raspberries on top of the chilled chocolate filling.
5. Brush the melted raspberry jam over the raspberries to glaze them.
6. Serve the raspberry chocolate tart chilled, and enjoy!

This raspberry chocolate tart is sure to impress your guests with its rich chocolate filling and vibrant raspberry topping. It's a perfect dessert for special occasions or anytime you're craving something indulgent and delicious.

Mixed Berry Bread Pudding

Ingredients:

- 6 cups of day-old bread, cubed (such as French bread or brioche)

- 2 cups mixed berries (such as strawberries, blueberries, raspberries, and blackberries), fresh or frozen
- 4 large eggs
- 2 cups whole milk
- 1/2 cup granulated sugar
- 1 teaspoon vanilla extract
- 1/2 teaspoon ground cinnamon
- Pinch of salt
- Butter, for greasing the baking dish

Instructions:

1. Preheat your oven to 350°F (175°C). Grease a 9x13-inch baking dish with butter.
2. Spread the cubed bread evenly in the prepared baking dish. Scatter the mixed berries over the bread.
3. In a mixing bowl, whisk together the eggs, whole milk, granulated sugar, vanilla extract, ground cinnamon, and a pinch of salt until well combined.
4. Pour the egg mixture over the bread and berries in the baking dish, making sure to evenly coat all the bread cubes.
5. Press down lightly on the bread cubes to help them absorb the liquid. Let the mixture sit for about 10-15 minutes to allow the bread to soak up the custard mixture.
6. Bake the bread pudding in the preheated oven for 45-50 minutes, or until the top is golden brown and the custard is set.
7. Remove the bread pudding from the oven and let it cool for a few minutes before serving.
8. Serve the mixed berry bread pudding warm, optionally topped with a scoop of vanilla ice cream or a drizzle of berry sauce.

Enjoy your delicious mixed berry bread pudding! It's a comforting and satisfying dessert that's perfect for any occasion, from cozy family dinners to special gatherings with friends. Feel free to customize the recipe with your favorite combination of berries or add a sprinkle of powdered sugar on top for extra sweetness.

www.ingramcontent.com/pod-product-compliance
Lightning Source LLC
LaVergne TN
LVHW062048070526
838201LV00080B/2208